Vickie

Mudlarks

B L O O M S B U R Y
LONDON • NEW DELHI • NEW YORK • SYDNEY

Bloomsbury Methuen Drama

An imprint of Bloomsbury Publishing Plc

50 Bedford Square   1385 Broadway

London   New York

WC1B 3DP   NY 10018

UK   USA

www.bloomsbury.com

Bloomsbury is a registered trade mark of Bloomsbury Publishing Plc

First published by Methuen Drama in 2012
Cover image by Alexander Henderson

© Vickie Donoghue 2012

Vickie Donoghue has asserted her right under the Copyright, Designs and
Patents Act 1988 to be identified as the author of this work

Visit www.bloomsbury.com to find out more about our authors and their books
You will find extracts, author interviews, author events and you can sign up for
newsletters to be the first to hear about our latest releases and special offers.

British Library Cataloguing-in-Publication Data
A catalogue record for this book is available from the British Library.

ISBN: PB: 978-1-4081-7303-9
EPDF: 978-1-4081-7305-3
EPUB: 978-1-4081-7304-6

Library of Congress Cataloging-in-Publication Data
A catalog record for this book is available from the Library of Congress.

 HighTide Festival Theatre

MUDLARKS

A new play by Vickie Donoghue

First performance at the HighTide Festival, Halesworth, Suffolk on 4 May 2012.

London premiere at Theatre503 on 29 May 2012.

A HighTide Festival Theatre and Lucy Jackson production.

Mudlarks was developed as part of HighTide Festival Theatre's Escalator Plays scheme.

A major initiative of the Old Possums Trust

MUDLARKS

A world premiere by Vickie Donoghue
A HighTide Festival Theatre and Lucy Jackson production

Jake	Scott Hazell
Charlie	James Marchant
Wayne	Mike Noble

Director	Will Wrightson
Designer	Amy Jane Cook
Lighting Designer	Joshua Carr
Composer and Sound Designer	Richard Hammarton
Stage Manager	Rebecca Day
Production Manager	Ben O'Neill
Fight Director	Paul Benzing
Producer	Lucy Jackson
Casting Director	Hayley Kaimakliotis
Assistant Producer	Chris Foxon
Design Assistant	Nick Spalding
Publicity Photography	Alexander Henderson

The producers would like to thank

Jerry Smith, The Angel of the North, Anthony Ratcliffe, Stephen Fry,
William Russell, Juliet Wrightson, Robert Gillespie and Anna Jackson,
Penelope Wrightson, Pamela Goold, Jamie Wrightson, Johnny White
Abbott, Watcyn Lewis, Ginny Henderson, Sir John Mactaggart, Sir Stephen
Waley Cohen, Betsy Bell, David and Susie Dugdale, William Eccles,
Isobel Tatham and Sam Gordon, Caroline Wilson, Aubrey Ayoade,
David Verey, Ashley Smatt, Bruichladdich, Fuller, Smith and
Turner Brewery, Felix Trench and Robert Bradley.

The production is supported by Arts Council East,
The Arts Patrons' Trust, The Mackintosh Foundation,
The Bacon Charitable Trust and the Unity Theatre Trust.

CAST

SCOTT HAZELL (JAKE)

Theatre includes *Masterclass* (Theatre Royal Bath/Chichester Festival Theatre), *Days Of Significance* (RSC) and *Junk* (Broadway Theatre).

Television includes *Law and Order UK*, *Alive!*, *Waking The Dead*, *The Bill* and *Primeval*.

Film includes T.S. Eliot *Flyboys* and *Croc*.

Scott was selected for the Old Vic UK/USA Exchange in 2010 in association with the Old Vic and the Public Theatre, NYC.

JAMES MARCHANT (CHARLIE)

Trained at Drama Centre London.

Theatre includes *The Straits* (Paines Plough, National tour and New York), *Perchance To Dream* (Finborough Theatre), *Three More Sleepless Nights* (Tristan Bates Theatre) and *The Seagull*, *Translations* and *All's Well That Ends Well* (Drama Centre).

Television includes *Criminal Justice*, *Waking The Dead*, *Surviving Disaster*, *The Bill*, *All About George*, *Lie With Me*, *Dream Team*, *Totally Frank* and *Blackbeard*.

Film includes *Lake Placid 3*.

James will be appearing as 'Sam' in *The Midnight Beast*, produced by E4/Warp Films.

MIKE NOBLE (WAYNE)

Trained at Drama Centre London.

Theatre includes *Punk Rock* (Lyric Theatre, Hammersmith), *Two Planks and a Passion*, *The Winter's Tale*, *Figaro Gets Divorced*, *The White Devil*, *Last Days of Don Juan*, *Ivanov* and *All My Sons* (Drama Centre).

Television includes *Prisoners' Wives*.

Film includes *World War Z*, *Private Peaceful*, *Gambit* and *Jadoo*.

COMPANY

VICKIE DONOGHUE (WRITER)

Vickie graduated from the MA in Creative Writing (Plays and Screenplays) at City University in September 2009. A rehearsed reading of her MA piece *Talk for England* took place at RADA in March 2010. Her first short play *One Last Wave* was one of the three finalists of the 2005 Windsor Fringe Marriott Award. She was Dramaturg for *The Caroline Carter Show* by Flick Ferdinando which premiered at the Edinburgh Festival Fringe in August 2011. She is currently writer in residence at If You Dare Productions. *Mudlarks* is her debut full length play.

WILL WRIGHTSON (DIRECTOR)

Will has produced and directed nationally and internationally. In 2010 he was Associate Director and Producer of a brand new Peter Nichols play (Lingua Franca) that began in London and transferred to New York. In the same year he was the Associate Director and Producer of Threshold for 19;29 Theatre Company which was nominated for a Total Theatre award and described as 'a journey of excitement, adventure and heartbreak' by the British Theatre Guide. Earlier in 2010 he directed a night of performance and poetry in the Sir John Soane museum which was candlelit for the occasion. He then went on to direct Mozart's The Magic Flute for the long established company Opera Integra. He recently assisted Christopher Morahan on his revival of The Caretaker starring Jonathan Pryce, which is currently on a US tour after a stint at the Adelaide Festival. He was HighTide's 2010 Resident Assistant Director.

AMY JANE COOK (DESIGNER)

Amy Jane Cook trained at Motley Theatre Design School.

Theatre includes: *65 Miles*, *Once Upon a Time in Wigan* (Hull Truck/Paines Plough), *Hamlet* (Maria Theatre, Young Vic), *66 Books*, *Flooded Grave* and *Where's my Seat?* (Bush Theatre), *The Water Engine* (Old Vic Tunnels), *The Pride* (BeMe Theatre, Munich), *The 8th* (Paines Plough), *A Midsummer Night's Dream* (Broadway Theatre), *W11* (Gate Theatre), *She Stoops To Conquer* (Hoxton Hall), *It's About Time* (Nabokov, Latitude Festival), *Love's Labour's Lost* (Guilford Castle), *Limehouse Nights* (Limehouse Town Hall), *Ignite* (Complicité/Artsdepot) and *Manor* (Soho Theatre/Tristan Bates Theatre).

Film includes: art direction for *Fred's Meat* (North London Film Awards).

Amy has been an event and installation designer for the Bush Theatre, the Nabokov Arts Club, Polka Theatre and at Standon Calling Festival. She is associate designer with Kandinsky Theatre Company and resident designer with Theatre6. *www.amyjanecook.com*

JOSHUA CARR (LIGHTING DESIGNER)

Joshua Carr trained at RADA in Lighting Design and Stage Electrics.

Lighting design for theatre includes: *Stage Fright* (Theatre Royal Bury St Edmunds), *Port Authority* (Southwark Playhouse), *Dick Whittington* (Stafford Gatehouse), *His Teeth* (Only Connect), *The Love of the Nightingale*, *Threepenny Opera*, *Antigone* and *A Clockwork Orange* (Fourth Monkey), *The Song of Deborah* (The Lowry, Salford), *The Shape of Things* (Soho Gallery), *Cinderella* and *Billy Elliot* (Young Actors Theatre), *Breathing Corpses* (Curving Road/Theatre Delicatessen) and *The Northerners* (Finborough Theatre).

Credits as production electrician include the 2011 HighTide Festival, *The Sea Plays* (Old Vic Tunnels), *The Painter* (Arcola Theatre), *The Maddening Rain* (Old Red Lion Theatre) and *The Hostage* (Southwark Playhouse).

Other work includes Assistant Lighting Designer on *Xerxes* (Royal Northern College of Music) and *Rose* (Pleasance Theatre), Programmer on *Cosi Fan Tuti* (The Royal College of Music), production electrician and assistant lighting designer on *Lake Boat* and *Prarie du Chien* (Arcola Theatre) and *Lidless* (Trafalgar Studios), chief electrician and assistant lighting designer on *Ditch* (Old Vic Tunnels), deputy chief electrician on *The Railway Children* (Waterloo) and assistant trainer on the British Council's Lighting Course Tunisia programme.

RICHARD HAMMARTON (SOUND DESIGNER)

Theatre includes: *The Pitchfork Disney* (Arcola Theatre), *Judgement Day* (The Print Room), *Edward II* and *Dr Faustus* (Royal Exchange Theatre, Manchester), *Persuasion* (Salisbury Playhouse), *Speaking in Tongues* (Duke of York's Theatre), *Ghosts* (Duchess Theatre), *Platform* (Old Vic Tunnels), *People at Sea*, *The Real Thing*, *Arsenic and Old Lace*, *Les Liaisons Dangereuse* and *The Constant Wife* (Salisbury Playhouse), *Pride and Prejudice* (Bath Theatre Royal/National Tour), *The Mountaintop* (Trafalgar Studios/ Theatre503), *Breakfast With Mugabe* (Ustinov Studio, Bath), *Some Kind of Bliss*, *World's End* and *Hello and Goodbye* (Trafalgar Studios), *The Rise and Fall of Little Voice* (Harrogate Theatre), *Raisin in the Sun* and *Six Characters Looking for an Author* (Young Vic), *Dealer's Choice* and *The Shooky* (Birmingham Rep), *The Lifesavers* (Theatre503/ Mercury Theatre, Colchester), *Same Same* and *Fixer* (Oval House) and *Ship of Fools*, *Salt Meets Wound* and *Inches Apart* (Theatre503).

TV and Film composition includes: *Agatha Christie's Marple*, *Wipeout*, *Sex 'n' Death*, *Rajan and his Evil Hypnotist* and *Raptured*.

TV and Film orchestration includes: *Primeval*, *Jericho*, *Agatha Christie's Marple*, *If I Had You*, *Take Me*, *Dracula*, *Silent Witness*, *The Ship*, *Alice Through The Looking Glass*, *Scenes of a Sexual Nature* and *The Nine Lives of Tomas Katz*.

REBECCA DAY (STAGE MANAGER)
Rebecca trained at Central School of Speech and Drama.

Theatre credits as stage manager include *Climate Week – Play in a Day*, *How The World Began*, *Lakeboat*, *Prairie du Chien* (Arcola Theatre), *The History of the Pomegranate* (Jackson's Lane), *A Watch in the Tunnel* (Shaw Theatre), *Pendley Shakespeare Festival* (Pendley Manor Hotel), *Old Vic New Voices* – Time Warner *Ignite 4 & 5* (Waterloo East), *Billy Elliot* (Rose Theatre, Kingston), *The Wild Goose Chase* (White Bear Theatre Club), *Shakespeare's Birth*day (Rose Theatre, Bankside), *Buried Child* (Upstairs at the Gatehouse), *Valentine's Day is Over* (Oliver's Village Café), *Silkworks* (Southwark Playhouse), *The Doctor's Daughter* (Minack Theatre) and *Pythonesque* (Edinburgh Festival).

Theatre credits as deputy and assistant stage manager include *Piñera Project* (Arcola Theatre), *Amphibians* (Bridewell Theatre), *Trisha Brown: Early Works* (TATE Modern), *Love, Love, Love* (Paines Plough placement) and *A Mad World* (CSSD).

BEN O'NEILL (PRODUCTION MANAGER)
Currently working as a draughtsman on the London 2012 Olympic ceremonies, Ben previously worked as a Project Manager for Flywire and the Rigging Partnership on rigging and automation for numerous West End musicals, films and music tours including *Shrek*, *Jersey Boys*, *Les Mis*, Take That's Progress Tour, and the most recent Harry Potter films. He also carried out theatre development work in venues like the Duke of York's Theatre, the NT Olivier, and for the RSC Transformation. Other roles include specialist scenery construction for SEL Live's *Platform* at the Old Vic Tunnels, designer for Open Door Enter's *Secret Garden* (site specific, Brighton Fringe), and production manager for CETT's *Klein Kunst II* at the Roundhouse Studio.

PAUL BENZING (FIGHT DIRECTOR)
Fight Direction includes: *Sweeney Todd* (Adelphi) *Journey's End* (Comedy Theatre), *Hamlet* (The Young Vic and the Nuffield Theatre Southampton), *Excuses* (Actors Touring Company), *National Anthem* (The Old Vic), *Lear* and *Who's Afraid of Virginia Woolf* (Crucible Theatre, Sheffield), *A Clockwork Orange*, *Son of Man*, *Look Back in Anger*, *Our Friends in The North* and *The Wind In The Willows* (Northern Stage), *The Country Wife*, *The Sea* and *Marguerite* (Theatre Royal, Haymarket). *Black Comedy, Treasure Island, Our Country's Good* and *Moonlight and Magnolias* (Watermill Theatre, Newbury), *What The Butler Saw* and *Beasts and Beauties* (Hampstead Theatre), *Oleanna* (Lakeside Arts, Nottingham), *The Comedy of Errors* and *Into The Woods* (Open Air Theatre, Regent's Park) and *Statement of Regret, Mother Courage, The Revenger's Tragedy, Nation, A Woman Killed with Kindness* and *Emperor and Galilean* (National Theatre).

LUCY JACKSON (PRODUCER)

Theatre includes: *Fanta Orange* and *Don Juan Comes Back From the War* at the Finborough Theatre, where she also produced all of the theatre's *Vibrant – A Festival of Finborough Playwrights* festivals (2009, 2010 and 2011). For Offstage Theatre Lucy produced *Amphibians* (Bridewell Theatre), for Misshapen Theatre she produced *Phillipa and Will are Now in a Relationship* and *The Sexual Awakening of Peter Mayo* (Pleasance Edinburgh and Theatre503) and *Blast Off* (Theatre503), and for Rogues' Gallery she produces The Folk Contraption (Heritage Arts Company VAULT Festival/ Priceless/London Wonderground/Latitude Festival). She was producer at Old Vic New Voices for *The 24 Hour Plays*, *The TS Eliot US/UK Exchange* (The Old Vic) and *Time Warner Ignite 4* (Waterloo East). She has produced and managed at six Edinburgh Festival Fringes including *White Rabbit, Red Rabbit* (Volcano Theatre) and *Thom Tuck Goes Straight-to-DVD* (Fosters Edinburgh Comedy Award Nominee for Best Newcomer). She has worked as a Production Assistant for TEG Productions/Jeremy Meadow Ltd.

HAYLEY KAIMAKLIOTIS (CASTING DIRECTOR)

Hayley is the Resident Casting Director for the Finborough Theatre, where her credits include *Don Juan Comes Back From The War, Foxfinder, Fanta Orange, Drama at Inish, Accolade, Me and Juliet, Love on The Dole, Miss Lilly Gets Boned, The Northerners* and three seasons of *Vibrant – A Festival of Finborough Playwrights*.

Other theatre credits include *The Firewatchers* (Old Red Lion Theatre), *A Midsummer Night's Dream* (Wirksworth Festival/Riverside Studios), *Amphibians* (Bridewell Theatre) and the forthcoming *Lizzie Finn* (Southwark Playhouse).

Casting assistant work for television includes *Casualty* and *Doctors*.

CHRIS FOXON (ASSISTANT PRODUCER)

Chris read English at Oxford University and trained at the Central School of Speech & Drama.

Producing includes *The Madness of George III* (Oxford Playhouse) and *This Is India* (O'Reilly Theatre).

Assistant producing includes *Don Juan Comes Back From The War* (Finborough Theatre), *Anastasia* (Pushkin House) and *On The Threshing Floor* (Hampstead Theatre).

Chris has also worked as a freelance sports journalist and has had articles published both in the UK and in India.

NICK SPALDING (DESIGN ASSISTANT)

Nick studied Sculpture at Brighton University and since graduating he has been designing and building sets for performance art and immersive installations, often concerned with interpretations of 'Paradise' or post-apocalyptic landscapes/nuclear winter.

Television credits include the art departments of Mister Maker, Horrible Histories Take Me Out and Big Brother.

Nick is currently constructing an art events space with a group of artists in South London.

 HighTide Festival Theatre

New Theatre For Adventurous Audiences

'Sharp, irreverent and fresh.' Daily Telegraph

HighTide Festival Theatre is a national theatre company and engine room for the discovery, development and production of exceptional new playwrights.

Under Artistic Director Steven Atkinson, the annual HighTide Festival in Suffolk has become one of the UK's leading theatre events, and in 2012 we are excited to premiere 18 new works. HighTide's productions then transfer nationally and internationally in partnerships that have included: the Bush Theatre (2008 & 2009), National Theatre (2009), Old Vic Theatre (2010), Ambassador Theatre Group / West End (2011), to the Edinburgh Festival (2008, 2010 & 2011) and internationally to the Australian National Play Festival (2010).

HighTide receives, considers and produces new plays from all around the world, every play is read and the festival is an eclectic mix of theatre across several venues in Halesworth, Suffolk. Our artistic team and Literary Department are proud to develop all the work we produce and we offer bespoke development opportunities for playwrights throughout the year.

HighTide Festival Theatre is a National Portfolio Organisation of Arts Council England.

A Brief History

The Sixth HighTide Festival in 2012

Luke Barnes, Jon Barton, Ollie Birch, Mike Daisey, Joe Douglas, Vickie Donoghue, Tom Eccleshare, Kenny Emson, Berri George, Karis Halsall, Nancy Harris, Ella Hickson, Branden Jacobs-Jenkins, Mona Mansour, Laura Marks, Ian McHugh, Jon McLeod, Shiona Morton Laura Poliakoff, Mahlon Prince, Stella Fawn Ragsdale, Stephanie Street, Philip Wells, Nicola Werenowska, Alexandra Wood

The sixth HighTide Festival in 2012 will premiere eighteen plays in world and European premiere productions in partnerships with emerging companies and leading theatres including: Bad Physics, curious directive, Escalator East to Edinburgh, Headlong, Halesworth Middle School, Latitude Festival, Lucy Jackson, macrobert, nabokov, The Nuffield Southampton, The Public Theater, Soho Theatre, Utter.

Ella Hickson's *Boys* will transfer to The Nuffield Theatre, Southampton and Soho Theatre in a co-production with the Nuffield Theatre, Southampton and Headlong.

Luke Barnes' Eisteddfod will transfer to the 2012 Latitude Festival.

Joe Douglas' *Educating Ronnie* will transfer to the 2012 Edinburgh Festival produced in association with macrobert and Utter.

Luke Barnes' *Bottleneck* will premiere at the 2012 Edinburgh Festival.

Charitable Support
HighTide is a registered charity (6326484) and we are grateful to the many organisations and individuals who support our work, including Arts Council England and Suffolk County Council.

Trusts and Foundations
The Bulldog Arts Fund, The Chivers Charitable Trust, The Coutts Charitable Trust, The DC Horn Foundation, The Eranda Foundation, The Ernest Cook Charitable Trust, Esmée Fairbairn Foundation, The Foyle Foundation, The Garrick Charitable Trust, The Genesis Foundation, IdeasTap, Jerwood Charitable Foundation, The Leche Trust, The Mackintosh Foundation, The Peggy Ramsay Foundation, Scarfe Charitable Trust, The Suffolk Foundation, SOLT/Stage One Bursary for New Producers, Harold Hyam Wingate Foundation, subsidised rehearsal space provided by Jerwood Space.

Business Sponsorship
ACTIV, AEM International, Ingenious Media Plc, Lansons Communications, Plain English.

Major Donors
Peter Fincham, Nick Giles, Bill and Stephanie Knight, Clare Parsons and Tony Langham, Tony Mackintosh and Criona Palmer, Albert Scardino, Peter Wilson MBE.

With thanks to all our Friends of the Festival

HighTide Festival Theatre, 24a St John Street, London, EC1M 4AY
HighTide Writers' Centre, The Cut, Halesworth, Suffolk, IP19 8BY

0207 566 9765
hello@hightide.org.uk
www.hightide.org.uk

Theatre503 is the home of fearless, irreverent, brave and provocative new plays. Working with the most important artists of today and discovering the foremost voices of tomorrow, we push at the boundaries of what theatre can be and pose the unanswerable questions of our time. Theatre503 has proudly premiered over 50 of the most exciting writers of our generation, including Dennis Kelly, Phil Porter, Duncan Macmillan, Rachael Wagstaff, Ali Taylor, Rex Obano and Lou Ramsden. In November 2006 Paul Robinson and Tim Roseman were appointed Artistic Directors. Their vision is to develop 503 as a crucible where writers, directors, actors and designers think better and bolder than they would expect. We seek out, nurture and promote work of uncommon and exceptional promise from artists both fresh off the boat and weathered with success. Since 2007 we have striven to become the most important theatre in the UK for first-time playwrights, providing that vital launchpad into public performance. The Mountaintop by Katori Hall started life at Theatre503 before transferring to the West End where it won the Olivier Award for Best New Play, the only time ever a theatre our size has been recognised this way. It opened in October 2011 on Broadway starring Samuel L. Jackson and Angela Bassett.

Artistic Directors - Tim Roseman and Paul Robinson
General Manager - Jeremy Woodhouse
Producer - Flavia Fraser-Cannon
Associate Director - Lisa Cagnacci
Literary Manager - Steve Harper
Literary Assistant - Kezia Cole
Resident Assistant Producers - Claire Turner and Lucy Pattison
503Five Resident Playwrights - Brad Birch, Jon Brittain,
Charlene James, Gemma Langford, Chris Urch
Senior Readers - Sarah Grochala, Alex Sims, Graeme Thompson
Young Creative Leaders Project Manager - Louise Abbotts
Development Director - Suzy Humphries
Development - Michael Levy, Marianne Powell, Jill Segal
Intern - Euan Borland
Affiliate Artists - Gene David Kirk, Lisa Spirling, Jessica Beck

Friends of Theatre503:
Annie Caird, David Chapman and Judy Molloy, Sue and Keith Hamilton, Amy Rotherham, Frankie Sangwin, Abigail Thaw, Mike and Hilary Tyrer, Charlie Westenra, Bernice Chitnis, Mike Morfey, Liz Padmore, Jill Segal, Penny Egan, Sandra Chalmers, Yve Newbold, Jerwood, Ponsonby, Andrew and Julia Johnson, Georgia Oetker, John Stokerson, Stuart Mullins, Kay Ellen Consolver, Cas Donald, Eileen Glynn, Deborah Shaw, Steve Marquardt, Kate Beswick, Jason Meininger, Craig Simpson, Lisa Forrell and Marisa Drew.

Mudlarks

For Lisa

Characters

Jake, *sixteen/seventeen years old*
Charlie, *sixteen/seventeen years old*
Wayne, *sixteen/seventeen years old*

Act One

It's the middle of the night on the Thames river wall in Essex. The tide is out so the mud is exposed. Lying on the mud is a rotten, upside-down rowing boat, a shopping trolley and lots of broken bottles.

Charlie *and* **Wayne** *jump off the wall and on to the mud.*

*They are both wearing football shirts (**Charlie** wears West Ham, **Wayne** wears Liverpool). **Wayne** wears a Liverpool bobble hat and a lady's handbag across his chest. They have been running hard, for a long time. They are out of breath and can't talk.*

They look at each other and burst out laughing.

Wayne   That was brilliant.

Charlie   I can feel me ticker banging in me chest.

Bang, Bang, Bang.

It's like it's congratulating me.

Wayne   Well done us! Well done us!

Charlie   We're so good!

Wayne   Oh god, I can't breathe.

Charlie   We are so fucking good!

Wayne   Me lungs have gone all small.

Charlie   We are the best!

Wayne   The fucking best!

Charlie   We actually dared to do something.

Wayne   That was something . . .

Charlie   And fucking did it.

Wayne   We did it!

Charlie   We are the fucking bollocks!

That was the best night I've had in ages.

He spits.

Wayne   Me too!

Charlie   What we just did, what we just did will go down in history. Who do you know that would have done that? Who would have had the guts?

Wayne   No one!

Charlie   We will be talked about.

Wayne   For ages!

Charlie   I feel like we could do anything now! Rule the world!

Wayne   Fucking kings!

Charlie   It felt so good didn't it?

Wayne   We just did it! Just like that!

Charlie   Just another day at the office!

Wayne   I can't believe we did it.

Charlie   I knew it would be a laugh.

Wayne   It was a laugh.

Charlie   We became legends tonight. It's one thing to think it, it's another to actually do it.

Wayne   I was running and running, but I couldn't breathe because I was laughing so much. I was laughing so hard a bit of wee came out.

Charlie   What a night.

Wayne   We have been busy boys.

Charlie   No. We've been men. We were real men tonight.

Wayne   I mean what didn't we do!

Charlie   We did everything!

Wayne   We did everything. (*Pause.*) Did we?

Charlie   What?

Wayne   We didn't do everything. We didn't do assault.

Did we? We didn't do nuffing like that.

Pause.

Did we?

Charlie *spits.*

Charlie   Nothing matters after what just happened. Not now. Not after what we just did.

Wayne   Well, I definitely didn't assault anyone. I didn't hurt anyone. I ain't done nuffing like that. I wouldn't hurt anyone.

Charlie   We didn't hurt anyone.

Wayne   Shit. Do you think we hurt someone?

Charlie   Can't think about it mate.

Wayne   Can't think about it.

Charlie   Just enjoy it!

Wayne   Just enjoy it.

Charlie   Enjoy the feeling!

Wayne   I'm enjoying the feeling.

They both pause.

Wayne   We probably did hurt someone though didn't we?

Charlie   Probably.

They both crack up laughing.

There is a noise above the river wall.

Wayne   What was that?

Charlie   Dunno.

They pause and listen.

Wayne   It's probably the docks.

Charlie   Yeah.

Wayne (*laughing*)   Don't shit yourself.

Charlie (*laughing*)   I ain't shitting meself.

Wayne   I do feel a bit weird though. Bit jumpy. I've been shaking . . . since we . . . aren't you shaking? It's the adrenalin thing innit . . . buzzing . . . Oh god . . . It was brilliant . . .

Wayne *is anxiously strutting up and down the mud. With the handbag on he resembles a woman.*

Charlie   Alright darling? Fancy meeting you 'ere.

Wayne   What?

Charlie   What the fuck . . .? Is that a handbag?

Wayne   Grabbed it off the back seat of the car we nicked.

Charlie   Borrowed.

Wayne (*laughs*)   Oh yeah, borrowed.

Charlie   Why you wearing it like a bird?

Wayne   It was easier to run wiv it like this. I can understand why girls get bags.

Charlie   What?

Wayne   Much better than carrying all your stuff in your pockets. Don't you think? Very . . . convenient.

Charlie   Why are you such a twat!

Wayne   It's a posh one! Thought there might be something in it.

Charlie   Come on then.

Charlie *grabs the handbag off* **Wayne** *and tips the contents out. A purse, lipstick, phone and a can of deodorant tumble on to the mud.*

Wayne   What you do that for? I stole it. I had the guts and cleverness to grab it and run wiv it for miles. I'm the one who bothered to look on the back seat.

I had to carry it all this way but you get to look through the stuff.

Charlie   Shut up. (*He spits.*)

Charlie *grabs the deodorant.*

Charlie   Yes! Biff that later!

Wayne   I thought you didn't do that any more.

Charlie   Only 'cause I can't get hold of any. Me 'old tits' moved to roll on, stupid bitch.

Wayne   Didn't you . . . you know . . . last time . . .

Charlie   Shut up.

Wayne   But you nearly . . .

Charlie   Who are you?

He puts the can in his pocket and grabs the purse.

Wayne   A wallet!

Charlie   Finder's keepers.

Wayne   Why can't something just be mine for once?

Wayne *goes to grab the purse back but* **Charlie** *pushes him over into the mud.*

Charlie   I said finder's keepers. Muppet.

Charlie *opens the purse and finds a ten-pound note. He puts it into his pocket. He takes out a driving licence.*

Charlie   Miss Louise Biss.

Wayne   Don't Charlie. It makes it real don't it.

Charlie (*looks at the picture*)   Cor she's ugly. Fat pig.

Wayne   Is she? Let's have a look.

Charlie *doesn't show him and throws the driving licence into the water.*

Wayne   She sounded nice. Biss. Louise. Pretty name.

Bag smells. Like perfume. Louise. Lou-ise. I wonder what she's like.

Charlie   You got a drink?

Wayne *ceremoniously pulls two cans of Stella out of his pocket.*

Wayne   Got two packets of crisps in me pocket as well and guess what? There was a box of fags in that bird's car as well! (*He holds up his supplies.*) We've got supplies to stay all night!

Charlie *takes a cigarette and lights it, takes a can of Stella for himself and a packet of crisps.*

Charlie   We're not staying here all night. What is wrong with you? This is a temporary situation.

Wayne   It will be like the old days when we used to camp all night in me garden. We can tell ghost stories. Light a fire. We can piss in the river.

Charlie   You are boring the fucking tits off me.

Charlie *starts eating a bag of crisps.*

Charlie   What flavour crisps are these?

Wayne   Cheese and onion.

Charlie   For fuck's sake. (*He spits them out.*)

Wayne *eats both packets of crisps as they sit and wait.*

Wayne   Cold innit!

Charlie   Wayne?

Wayne   Yeah?

Charlie   Name a Liverpool football player that ain't Steven Gerrard.

Silence as he thinks.

Wayne   Fuck off!

Charlie (*laughing*)   I love it that you can't name any!

Wayne   Just 'cause West Ham are shit.

Charlie   Why d'you support Liverpool again?

Wayne   'Cause my dad.

Charlie (*laughs*)   And how is your dad?

Wayne   Fuck off.

Charlie   Sorry.

Charlie *gets a text message.*

Charlie   You sure no one saw us run down here?

Wayne   I was just concentrating on me running Charlie.

Charlie   Bell end.

Wayne   I'm rubbish at running.

Charlie   Why'd we come down here? It's horrible.

Wayne   Don't you remember it?

Charlie   No.

Wayne   We used to come down here all the time.

Charlie   It's shit.

Wayne   It's the best place to hide. Ever.

Charlie   Fucking stinks.

Wayne   I come down here a lot. To think.

Charlie   What the fuck have you got to think about?

Wayne *can't think of anything.*

Charlie   Only the scum of the earth hang out down here. Look at it. Fucking needles and cans.

Wayne   I quite like it.

Charlie   You would.

Wayne   Come down here on a Sunday. It's not all druggies, who's done all the graffiti then?

Charlie   What, that shit along the walls?

Wayne   Every artist /

Charlie   Artist!

Wayne   . . . has certain sections of the riverwall and they all respect it and don't spray over each other's.

Charlie   Pricks. I would.

Charlie *gets a text message.*

Wayne   Don't you think it's good? (*Pause.*) Charlie?

Charlie   What you banging on about?

Wayne   The graffiti.

Charlie   It's shit.

Wayne   It's amazing!

Charlie   It's a waste of time. No one can see it down here.

Wayne   They draw so quickly. Every line counts. I'm well jealous of them. I stole a few of the empties that were thrown on the grass, still had a bit in them so I had a go on the wall in the garden. I was well shit. It's really hard.

Charlie   What do you sound like?

Wayne   I wish I could do it that's all. How cool to be that amazing at something. Imagine –

Charlie*'s mobile phone rings.*

Charlie   Shit.

Wayne   You alright Charlie?

Charlie   Tonight was meant to be a laugh.

Wayne   It is a laugh. You ate cheese and onion and you hate cheese and onion. That was pretty funny.

Charlie   Just wasn't meant to . . . I didn't think . . .

Wayne   What you talking about?

Charlie's *mobile phone rings.*

Wayne   Who is it?

Charlie   No one.

Wayne   Who's no one?

Charlie   No one.

Wayne   Why you being weird?

The sound of footsteps.

Charlie (*whispers*)   Did you hear that?

Wayne (*whispers*)   Someone's followed us down here.

Charlie   Fuck . . .

Wayne   Someone must have saw what we did.

No one normally comes down here Charlie.

Honestly. I'm sorry, Charlie.

Charlie   I knew they'd find us.

Wayne   Who's up there? What's going on? Do you know who's up there?

Charlie   I didn't even do anything.

Wayne   Who is it?

Charlie   This ain't my fault.

The footsteps are getting nearer and nearer.

Wayne   Shit. Oh shit. What we going to do?

Charlie   Stop panicking.

Wayne   Oh god. Oh god. There's someone up there?

Charlie   Stop talking then.

Wayne   Shit. Shit. Shit.

Charlie   Do you want to get caught?

Wayne   Who's up there Charlie?

Charlie   Do. You. Want. To. Get. Caught?

Wayne   No.

Charlie   Well, shut the fuck up then.

Charlie and **Wayne** *fling themselves up against the riverwall so that they are just out of sight.*

Wayne   Caught by who?

Charlie's *mobile phone rings. He quickly stops it.*

Wayne   Why does your phone keep ringing?

Charlie   Shhhh.

Wayne   What have you done, Charlie?

Charlie   Shhhhh!

Wayne (*whispering*)   Did something happen at the pool hall?

Charlie   Shut up!

Wayne   I was standing out there for ages. The pool hall? Who do you even know in the –

(*Pause.*)

(*Whispers.*) Someone is definitely up there. I can hear them breathing.

Charlie (*whispers*)   Well stop fucking talking then.

Wayne   Yeah but /

Charlie *covers* **Wayne**'s *mouth up with his hand.*

Suddenly, **Jake** *jumps off the riverwall and falls on to the wet mud.*

Wayne   Jake! Oh god. Jake! You alright?

Charlie   Is he hurt?

Wayne   You hurt, Jake? You alright? Oh god. Where you been?

Charlie   Thought you'd gone home.

Wayne   We've been worried.

Charlie   I ain't been worried.

Wayne   We thought you'd been caught?

Charlie   No we didn't.

Wayne   What happened?

Charlie   Yeah, what happened?

Wayne   We just ran and ran. Didn't look back, did we?

Charlie   Should have stayed with us mate. Going off on your own . . .

Wayne   Thought we'd lost you.

Charlie   Thought you'd gone home to mummy.

Wayne   I didn't know if you'd remember down here.

Jake *runs over to the water and is violently sick.*

Charlie   What's the matter with you?

You fucking girl!

Wayne   Urggh, that stinks.

Charlie   You great big fucking girl!

First he runs like one now he's puking like one.

Wayne   It always makes you feel like you're going to be sick don't it?

Charlie   Not pregnant are ya?

Wayne   Oh god, I do feel a bit sick now!

Charlie   Why you being sick?

Jake *can't speak.*

Wayne   I think I'm gonna puke!

Jake *slumps down on to the mud holding his stomach.*

Charlie   I said, why you being sick?

Wayne   Leave him, Charlie!

Charlie   What's going on, Jake? Where you been? Why were you so far behind? Come on!

Wayne   You did take ages.

Jake *is shivering.*

Wayne   You alright, Jake?

Jake *nods.*

Wayne   Do you want my coat, Jake?

Jake *shakes his head.*

Charlie (*in a girl's voice*)   Do you want my coat, Jake? Do you actually have testicles?

Wayne   Something's wrong, Charlie.

Charlie's *mobile phone rings. He quickly stops it.*

Charlie   Get him up. We need to run.

Wayne   We can't. I mean, where would we go?

Charlie   Somewhere else, numbnuts!

Wayne   Where, Charlie?

Charlie   I don't know.

Wayne   But you said we had to hide.

Charlie   Think!

Wayne   I like it here. I like hiding.

Charlie   We need to keep moving. We can't just sit here.

Wayne   Someone's after him, Jake.

Charlie   Mind ya own.

Wayne   Is it Kirsty?

Charlie   Don't mention her name ever again.

Wayne   I've never liked her.

Charlie   That word don't cross your skanky lips.

Wayne   Never known what you see in her.

Charlie   We're like fucking prey sat down here.

Wayne   She's not good enough for you.

Charlie   Shut up.

Wayne   Just saying . . .

Charlie*'s mobile phone rings. He quickly stops it.*

Charlie   Shit. My dad would know what to do.

Wayne (*excited*)   I wanna stay all night!

Charlie   We are not staying here all night. Especially with you keeping on.

Wayne   We can't go home. I mean we shouldn't go home. Not yet. Tell him, Jake. We should wait a bit.

Charlie   You scared of going home or something?

Wayne   I ain't scared.

Charlie   You should be more scared of what's up there mate.

Wayne   Why would your dad know what to do? Who's up there? What's going on? Why should we be scared?

Charlie   For fuck's sake, you're getting on my nerves. Tonight was about having fun. Doing something we'd never done before and look what it's turned into. The most boring night ever!

Jake *slumps on to the mud exhausted.*

Charlie *goes over to where* **Jake** *is.*

Charlie   And you're getting on my tits. Say something.

Jake *can't speak.*

Charlie   Weren't much help tonight were you?

Wayne   Yeah! You weren't much help, Jake?

Charlie   Why didn't you help?

Wayne   Yeah, why didn't you help, Jake?

Charlie   We asked you a question. Jake? Jake?

Charlie *kicks* **Jake** *hard.* **Jake** *shrieks.*

Wayne   It was fucking heavy.

Charlie   Only cos he didn't help.

Wayne   Did you hear the noise it made . . . you know . . . when it . . . you know . . . it was horrible!

Jake *is violently sick again.*

Charlie (*cross*)   Why do you keep being sick? What the fuck's going on Jake! What's going on? Stop fucking being sick! Fucking say something or I'm going to fucking hurt you.

Wayne   Charlie . . .

Charlie   Fuck off.

Wayne   Please say something, Jake.

Charlie   Say something you mug.

Why ain't you saying anything?

Charlie *kicks* **Jake** *again. Hard.* **Jake** *is more prepared for it this time.*

Charlie   You were there, you're part of this.

Just cos your little girl hands didn't actually touch it. Say something?

You didn't stop us. You are part of this.

Fucking say something!

Pause.

Jake (*takes a big breath*)   The p. . .p. . .pigs!

Wayne   Where?

Jake   Everywhere.

Wayne   Are they coming down here?

Jake   They were everywhere.

Wayne   Shit. Oh shit. What we going to do?

Charlie   Stop panicking.

Wayne   Oh god. Oh god.

Charlie   We don't know that they are looking for us.

Wayne   We get caught this time. That will be it. Someone must have seen us.

Charlie   No one saw us and even if they did what are they actually gonna do?

His mobile phone rings. He quickly stops it.

Fucking hell! I can't sit on this mud all night.

Wayne   We can't risk it. They'll nick you for something you know they will.

Charlie   I ain't scared of 'em. (*He looks at his phone.*) Just need to get this sorted.

Wayne   Get what sorted Charlie?

Charlie   What is wrong with you two? You're useless.

His mobile phone rings again.

For fuck's sake!

He throws it into the water.

Wayne   I can't believe you just threw your mobile into the water!

Charlie   I can't sit here all night with you two. Snivelling like babies.

Wayne   I'd have had it.

Charlie   I need to see for myself.

Wayne   What's going on Charlie?

Charlie   I'm going to look.

Wayne   Charlie!

Charlie   What?

Wayne   Be careful.

Charlie   Fuck off!

He climbs up and over the riverwall and disappears into the darkness.

Wayne   I can't believe he threw his phone in the water!

Pause.

You alright, mate?

Still feel sick?

Don't want to talk about it right?

Well whatever happens, it was a laugh. Right?

Pause.

Sure you're alright?

Pause.

Jake   What the fuck have we done?

Wayne   Nothing. We ain't done nothing. Don't stress.

Jake   But the police . . .

Wayne   They probably won't bother coming all the way down here mate. They're dinlos!

Jake   I just ran and ran and ran . . .

Wayne   How did you know we'd be here?

Jake   Legs just took me here.

Wayne   I knew you'd remember!

Jake   Kept falling over. Just ran and ran . . .

Wayne   Remember playing war down here? The boat was a tank.

Jake   . . . there were blue flashing lights everywhere . . .

Wayne   Get over it, mate. You're not the first person to be made a mug of. I haven't forgotten about when you and Charlie left me playing hide and seek and you two went home while I was hiding. I was there till it went dark.

Jake   It's bad. It's really bad.

Wayne   I was only eight. And I got over it. (*Pause.*) You and Charlie. Always whispering and planning things.

Jake   Why did you two have to . . . why did you . . .

Wayne   S'pose it's like when I set the bin on fire in me garden. I was bored so I burnt the plastic tray me dinner came in. It went woof, right up, didn't expect it to do that, didn't know what to do, so I threw it on to the lid of the wheelie bin. Melted right through the lid. Started setting on fire the rubbish inside. Me Dad went 'What did you do that for!' Clipped me round the head. I said 'I just wanted to see what would happen.'

Jake   Just wanted to see what had happened.

Wayne   Don't worry about it. We'll be fine. Me, you and Charlie have got in much more scrapes than this before.

Jake   I haven't.

Wayne   Well, me and Charlie have.

Jake   We are in serious, serious trouble.

Wayne   It weren't that bad.

Jake   I can't get caught.

Wayne   We won't get caught. I don't know why they're up there but they'll give up eventually. They'll have to go back and get their sandwiches soon. Report back to the station. Honestly, no one knows about this bit of beach.

Jake   It ain't a beach.

Wayne   Yeah it is.

Jake   It is not a beach.

Wayne   It's on the signs.

Jake   It ain't a beach.

Wayne   Well, everyone calls it that.

Jake   Doesn't make it a beach.

Wayne   Just cause there's no bucket and spades or people sunbathing.

Jake   This ain't the sea. It's a river.

Wayne   So what. We still call it a beach. Everyone does.

Jake   Did you learn anything at school?

Wayne   No.

They sit in silence.

Jake   Why's he gone up there?

Wayne   He's gone to have a look /

Jake   He'll get spotted, the police will come down here, and then . . .

Wayne   You know when you put a washing machine on?

Jake (*no answer*)

Wayne   How'd you know what setting to put it on?

Jake   How the fuck am I meant to know that?

Wayne   Alright! Only asking.

Seriously mate is everything OK?

Jake (*can't answer*)

Wayne   You and bloody Charlie. Doing my head in. Something's happening. His phone just kept going. Can't believe he threw it in the water.

Pause.

Did you know that putting coloured clothes in with your whites does actually ruin your clothes? It is not an urban myth!

Jake   Ain't your dad doing your washing any more?

Wayne (*pause*)   Why don't we go swimming any more?

Jake   We got banned.

Wayne   I loved going swimming with you two. We climbed up to the very top diving board and lay flat so no one could see us.

Jake   Do you think Charlie will be long?

Wayne   We waited till everyone had left the pool and the lifeguards were doing one last check before closing . . .

Jake   Don't, Wayne.

The old boat has become the diving board. **Wayne** *jumps up and down on it.*

Wayne   Then we took off our trunks, jumped up and down in the buff, swung them round our heads . . . and jumped into the pool!!!

Jake *starts laughing.*

Jake   The lifeguards shit themselves.

Wayne   It was brilliant. (*Pause.*) Perhaps we could go swimming this weekend?

Jake   We're too old. Too old for bombing nans and pissing in our trunks.

Pause.

Wayne   Do you know why I called you tonight?

Jake   Bored?

Wayne   I was stood outside the pool hall waiting for Charlie and I thought to myself . . . I really miss Jake.

Jake   Fuck off.

Wayne   I wish we could just get on our bikes and bomb around the town centre on a Saturday.

Jake   You didn't bomb round. Your chain was always coming off.

Wayne   It was a bit shit but I loved that bike.

Jake   We should be driving by now.

Wayne   We'd get chips. Mmm I bloody love chips. You and Charlie chipped up that traffic warden.

Jake   No we never.

Wayne   Yes you did.

Jake   Wouldn't hurt anyone though would we.

Wayne   Nick some Star Wars figures from the toyshop.

Jake   I hated doing that. I couldn't play with them. Felt too guilty looking at them.

Wayne   You loved that toyshop though. You was always eyeing up the metal detectors!

Jake   Stop it, Wayne.

Wayne   You really wanted one didn't you? Did you get one in the end? Charlie wanted a catapult. I wanted a whoopee cushion! I would go in there, pick it up and read the instructions on it until I knew them off by heart. The day Charlie stole one for me was the best day ever. I hate school but I skipped all the way there that day. I knew exactly what teacher's arse I was going to put it under. Mr Merrick. Flakey, Shakey Merrick. Did you ever have him? He was so horrible. I was pissing meself as he sat down in slow motion and the noise that came out of my whoopee cushion was bigger and better and louder than I could have imagined. It was perfect. It was the kind of fart that sounded like he'd shit himself. I was crying with laughter. Confiscated. One week's detention. But that week was worth it because I would just remember that noise that came from Mr Merrick's arse cheeks and I would be off again. I'm telling you Jake, you missed out on a whole heap of fun getting moved up a set.

Jake   I'm sorry I haven't been out as much lately.

Pause.

Wayne   I love it down here. I like all the twinkling lights. Reminds me of Southend. The arcades.

Jake   S'pose.

Wayne   I love the arcades. Remember when your mum took us to Southend, Jake? We went for the day. We had a Pizza Hut. Went to the aquarium.

Jake   Did we?

Wayne   You could see France across the water.

Jake   Do you still believe you could see France?

Wayne   Yeah.

Jake   You can't see France from Southend. It was Kent.

Wayne   Shut up.

We went in your mum's new car.

Big and warm and smelt of leather.

Jake   Till you puked up in it.

Wayne   That was that eat as much as you can buffet.

Jake   It was eat as much as you like.

Wayne   You got to get your money's worth.

Jake   Not so you puke.

Wayne   Yeah you do.

Pause.

I didn't know when I would get grub like that again.

Jake   That was the last time she took you and Charlie in her car.

Wayne   I liked the trips out with your mum, Jake.

Jake   Well, you fucked that up!

Pause.

Wayne   When Charlie gets back and the pigs have gone, why don't we bunk the train to Southend? Go Peter Pan's, the aquarium. Get a Pizza Hut.

Jake   We ain't going anywhere, mate. We ain't going anywhere for a long time.

Wayne   But we'll go back there one day?

Jake   Maybe.

The sound of footsteps. Someone is approaching.

Jake *and* **Wayne** *freeze.*

Jake (*whispers*)   Did you really miss me?

Wayne (*whispers*)   No. I was just bored.

Jake (*whispers*)   You missed me!

Wayne (*whispers*)   I didn't! Charlie was just in there for ages!!

Jake (*whispers*)   I need to tell you something.

Wayne (*pause*)   Are you going to be sick again?

Jake (*whispers*)   Tonight has ruined everything.

Wayne (*whispers*)   Ruined what?

Jake (*whispers*)   I've got plans.

Wayne (*whispers*)   Plans?

Jake (*whispers*)   I've made plans.

Wayne (*whispers*)   What plans?

Jake (*whispers*)   I can't change them.

Wayne (*whispers*)   We don't make plans.

Jake (*whispers*)   Sorted stuff out.

Wayne (*whispers*)   What you talking about mate?

Charlie *jumps from the seawall on to the mud. He does a roll as he lands.*

Wayne   Did you see that?! You should do that free running thing! You'd be well good.

Charlie   We have to go. We have to go now.

Wayne   We can't, Charlie.

Jake   Are they coming down here?

Charlie   Who?

Jake   The police.

Charlie   Stop pissing ya knickers about the police.

Wayne   We have to wait here until they're gone.

Jake   Why?

Charlie   It ain't safe to stay here.

Jake   What's going on?

Charlie   We need to keep on the move.

Wayne   Can't.

Charlie   What?

Wayne   Can't.

Jake   What do you mean, can't.

Wayne   No way out of here.

Jake   What?

Wayne   I'm sorry. We go up and face the pigs . . . or we . . . swim over there.

Charlie   What?

Jake   Can't we go along the beach?

Wayne   Factories and fencing.

Jake   This is a fucking mess.

Charlie   You took us down a dead end?

Wayne   I'm sorry Charlie.

Charlie   You prick.

Wayne   We'll be alright . . .

Jake   How are we going to be alright? The police are just up there!

Wayne   But we ain't done nothing wrong.

Jake   We're bloody trapped down here. I can't believe this. I can't believe this, Wayne!

Charlie   Don't shout at him!

Jake   We're bloody trapped!

Charlie   I said don't shout at him.

Wayne   We'll just have to wait until the pigs have gone.

Charlie   Need to think. Just need to think.

Pause.

Jake   Why are you so desperate to move?

Wayne   What you thinking about? Why'd you need to think?

Jake   Why's he shitting himself?

Charlie   I ain't shitting me self.

Wayne   You shitting yourself, Charlie?

Jake   What's going on?

Charlie   I'm not shitting myself!

Jake   What's going on? Tell me, Charlie.

Pause.

Charlie   Kirsty's brothers is what's going on.

Wayne   Kirsty's brothers . . . no . . . they're horrible, Charlie.

Jake   Jesus Christ . . .

Wayne   I thought you said it weren't assault?

Jake   What assault?

Charlie   It weren't assault.

Wayne   Something happened at the pool hall.

Charlie   Nothing happened at the pool hall.

Wayne   You came storming out of there.

Charlie   Why don't you shut your mouth?

Jake   What have you done Charlie? Fucking hell the pigs are going to have a field day.

Charlie   I don't give a flying fuck about the pigs. If Kirsty's brothers come down here, if they find us, then we are in serious fucking bother.

Charlie *sits on the old boat. He gets the can of deodorant and starts inhaling it.*

Jake   Did you hurt her?

Wayne   You sure you should be doing that, Charlie?

Charlie   I hit, no, no, no, no it weren't a hit, it was a push really, I pushed . . . Kirsty . . . whose brothers clearly don't like it very much. So what?

Wayne   You hit Kirsty!?

Charlie   You stole a handbag off a girl, what's the difference?

Wayne   You hit a girl!?

Jake   Charlie, what happened?

Charlie   I don't want to . . .

Wayne   I'm sure he didn't mean it.

Charlie   Can we all just . . .?

Wayne   You don't hit a girl. Unless she's been really annoying. I mean really winding you up.

Charlie *is now intoxicated. His voice is slower.*

Charlie (*rambling*)   She's amazing.

Wayne   She's not. She's got funny hair.

Charlie   She'd like it down here. Romantic if you squint. Next to the water. She's been texting me for days. She kept me up all last night. Text, kip, text, kip. I'd be floating off to sleep when the whole room would light up from the little tiny screen. 'You are a cock.' (*Laughs.*) Eyes closing, but text back 'You stink.'

Jake   Very romantic.

Charlie   Oh yeah, these weren't sweet nothings. They were cold hard cusses. I loved it.

When I got up this morning I sat on the sofa watching me dad stagger round looking for his shoes.

'How do you know if a girl likes yer, Dad?'

He growled 'You don't. They tell ya nuffing. Get used to it' That ain't true though is it?

Is that true? Is that true? Girls . . .

Wayne   I don't know mate. Sounds a bit harsh.

Charlie   We will never really know if they . . .?

Wayne   I hate girls.

Charlie   It ain't true.

Wayne   But your dad said so. He don't get nothing wrong.

Charlie   No one tells me the truth. They tell me what they think I want to hear but . . .

She had been telling me the truth all night. She was being more honest to me than anyone has ever been to me my whole life. 'You're a joke' she texted. Fucking amazing. I love it. Who else would have the fucking guts to call me 'a joke' to me face.

Wayne   No one.

Charlie *inhales from the can again and slumps to the ground.*

Jake   Is he alright?

Charlie   She's beautiful.

Wayne   Oh yeah, this is just what happens. It will wear off quick. Ain't you ever done it?

Jake   No.

Wayne   It is amazing, although it gives me the shits.

Jake   Not great at sharing is he.

Charlie   But she's a piss taker. Took it too far. Joke weren't that funny any more. She didn't know when to leave it. Tonight. Up at the . . . up at the . . . the . . .

Wayne   Pool hall.

Charlie   Pissed out her head. Having a go. She kept having a go. I let it go and I let it go and I let it go. I let it go. I let it go. (*He inhales again.*) I went outside. Get some air but she followed me. She's fucking beautiful. Fucking beautiful.

Wayne   Never knew you felt like that about her. You've never said before.

Charlie   Knew she was gagging for it. I grabbed her. Her dark hair. Scraped off her soft face. Held her hard. Tried to . . . I put my hands on her . . .

But she was screaming . . . and screaming . . .

Shouting and shouting.

Screaming like one them pit bulls.

Dig, dig, dig, dig, dig. Taking the piss.

It's no excuse. She just shouldn't have . . .

Shouldn't have pushed me in my face. My face. Shouldn't have done it. End of.

Now I'm here feeling like a twat and they're probably all talking about me and saying what a cunt I am. Shit. I don't know . . . I thought she . . .

Jake   What did you do to her?

Charlie   I knew something like this . . .

She's the type, you know. An aggro bird.

Finks she's funny. Finks she's . . .

What was I meant to do? I'm not a mug.

I ain't no . . . (*He can't remember the word. He inhales the can again but there is none left.*)

What are you meant to do, just take it?

Stand there and . . . and . . . I ain't havin' it.

This is her fault. You don't mess wiv me. (*Shouts.*) You don't mess wiv me!

I ain't a fucking coward. I'm not apologising neither. No. No way. I'm not having it. If you push me in the face, you get a shuv. If you are a girl, or if you are a boy, if you push me, IN MY FACE, you get a shuv. No, no, no I didn't hit her. I DID NOT HIT HER.

Jake   Shhh, Charlie! The pigs will hear us!

Charlie   I pushed her. Not that hard, but she fell over. Shit. I can't help that. But she hit me face, mate. It was a reaction. I reacted. I can't take it back. It happened. It has happened. She just looked at me. Looked up at me. With those eyes. Shit.

They're going to kill me. Those brothers will cut me up.

Jake This is a fucking nightmare. So, not only have we got the pigs after us we've got the fucking chuckle brothers chasing us.

Charlie And don't tell me to fucking shhh. Who do you think you are? You're not the fucking boss of me.

Jake We can't stay here. We can't just stay here after what we've done.

Charlie *gets a knife out of his pocket.*

Jake What the . . .

Charlie We're going to be alright.

Wayne Yes!

Jake Is this some kind of joke?

Charlie You need to calm down.

Jake Why have you got a fucking knife?

Wayne Have you met Kirsty's brothers?

Jake The pigs are just up there somewhere and you get a fucking knife out.

Wayne Wish I had one.

Jake This ain't us.

Charlie Yes it is. Yes it is Jake.

Wayne Can I hold it?

Jake Throw it in the water, Charlie. Or I will.

Charlie If you touch it . . . If you touch my knife . . .

Jake Throw it in the water.

Charlie No.

Wayne What's it feel like?

Jake I can't believe this is happening. Since when have we needed a knife?

Charlie   It's the way it is. Who's going to look after us?

Wayne   No one.

Charlie   What you going to do when those boys get down here, Jake? Talk them out of hurting us? We have to look after ourselves. After each other.

Jake   We don't need a knife.

Charlie   This is who we are now. This is what we do. But then, you wouldn't know that.

Jake   This isn't who I am.

Charlie   Where you been? Not on the streets. Where you been? Not with us. You ain't been out here.

Wayne   He's our mate, Charlie.

Charlie   He ain't our mate. We ain't seen him in months.

Why'd you text him tonight? Why'd you even bother with this piece of shit?

Jake   This ain't me.

Charlie   You think you're so much better than us don't you?

Jake   This ain't me.

Charlie   Yes it is.

Wayne   Everyone has 'em, Jake.

Jake   It ain't me.

Wayne   It's the way it is.

Charlie   It's a defence. A shield.

Wayne   It's a shield, Jake.

Charlie   I'm not actually gonna use it.

Wayne   Yeah, we're not actually gonna use it.

The sound of police sirens passing by in the distance.

Jake   I can't get caught by the police, Charlie.

Charlie   Why can't you get caught?

Wayne   We didn't do anything wrong.

Charlie   You scared of the police?

Jake   You have to tell them you did it.

Charlie   Don't tell me what to do, prick.

Jake   You have to tell them it wasn't me.

Charlie   You should feel proud of what we've done tonight. Stand tall. We can talk about this for years to come. Who else would have done it?

Jake   You can change this.

Charlie   We can't change this. We can't change nothing.

Jake   You can change how tonight ends. Put the knife down.

Wayne   Shit just happens, mate.

Charlie   Why don't you fuck off? Do one. Go and do whatever it is you've been doing for all these months without us. You're pathetic. Hiding away indoors. Sat in watching the fucking History Channel.

Wayne   Do you watch the History Channel?

Jake   Fuck off. Just fuck off.

Charlie *pushes* **Jake** *and puts the knife to his throat.*

Charlie   Tell Wayne what you been doing.

Jake   I ain't done nothing wrong.

Charlie   I saw your mum, Jake. I know everything.

Wayne   Why am I the last to know anything . . .

Charlie   Tell him!

Jake   I can't . . .

I can't do it.

Pause.

Charlie   He's leaving us.

Wayne   You ain't leaving.

Jake   I'm . . . I've been . . . I'm trying to . . .

Charlie *takes the knife from* **Jake**'s *throat and starts laughing.*

Charlie   Prick.

Wayne   You can't leave us.

Jake   I got a letter.

Wayne   What about me and Charlie?

Charlie   You ain't going anywhere. I told your mum. You're full of shit.

Jake   Kirsty's brothers and all this shit . . . you'll have to . . . it will be . . . it will be just you and Charlie. I won't . . . I won't be around.

Wayne   What do you mean? No one else is leaving. You can't just leave us. Tell him Charlie.

Charlie   You're nothing.

Jake   I want to be someone.

Charlie   No roads out of here, mate. It's a dead end this town.

Wayne   But you're one of us.

Charlie   No he's not. He's no one. You're no one 'cause you just stood there. Up on the bridge. Just stood there. Like a little boy. Shitting yourself.

Wayne   You did just stand there, Jake.

Charlie   You didn't even help.

Wayne   I didn't think we were going to get it up on to the railing without you. Took ages. Wobbling. Couldn't balance it.

Charlie   Just stood there.

Wayne   But then it was up . . . it was so good . . . balanced on the railing. Holding it there . . . for a second . . . with our fingers.

Charlie   And then . . .

Wayne   And then . . .

Charlie   We let go.

Wayne   It felt like . . . when it left our hands . . . it just flew. Didn't it. Like it went all light.

Charlie   It just shot straight down!

Jake   Stop it.

Charlie   We just let go . . . and . . .

Wayne   It went! It just went!

Charlie   Down. Down. Down into the darkness.

Wayne   Whooshing down. Down. Down. Crack!

Jake   Stop it.

Charlie   And it cracked. It fucking cracked.

Wayne   I ain't heard anything make that noise before!

It hit something. It definitely hit something 'cause of that noise. It made a horrible noise. I think I heard glass smash. Did you hear the glass smash?

Jake   I heard the glass smash.

Charlie   Stood there like a little boy.

Jake   I heard people screaming.

Charlie   Why are you here with us?

Wayne   Yeah, why are you still hiding, Jake?

Charlie   We don't want you here.

Wayne   Yeah! Don't we?

Charlie   Why can't you go? (*Pause.*) Go on. Fuck off.

Wayne   I think you should go, Jake.

Charlie   He can't go.

Why can't you go!!

I said, why can't you go?

Pause.

Jake   I looked.

Charlie   What?

Jake   I looked.

I ran over and looked over the side.

Charlie   You did what?

Pause.

Jake   The traffic had slowed.

Some cars had bumped into each other.

People were getting out.

Charlie   It don't matter.

Jake   People were shouting for help.

Charlie   I don't care.

Jake   I couldn't move. Couldn't run to catch you up. Stuck.
Just stood there. Listening. People were screaming. Crying.

So . . . I looked over a bit more.

Wayne   What . . . what did we hit Jake?

Charlie   It doesn't matter what we hit. It doesn't matter.

Jake   It was a lorry.

We hit a lorry.

They stand in silence. Stunned by what they've done.

Charlie   So? So what. That's what we wanted to do.

Wayne   Was it? Did we . . . I mean . . .

Charlie   It was a laugh. That's what we wanted.

Wayne   Yeah. It was a laugh, Jake.

Jake   I felt it. I felt the lorry hit the bridge.

I could see it had sort of spun.

Facing the wrong way in the middle of the . . .

I wanted to know. I needed to see.

So . . . I edged over further.

Windscreen smashed right through.

The cab was full of glass.

The man had come out a bit through the windscreen.

His arm . . . his arm was hanging down . . . out the front of the cab . . . not moving . . .

Not moving.

Wayne   Not moving?

Jake   It looked like a bit of meat.

Wayne   Not moving?

Jake   I edged over further. Blood. Lots of blood.

Wayne   Oh god.

Jake   I edged over further. There it was.

In the middle of the road.

Our bit of . . . the big concrete . . .

Wayne   You should have run, Jake. You should have stayed with us.

Jake   Me hands were frozen gripped round the railing.

He was wearing jeans. Horrible dad jeans.

He was listening to the radio.

He had been eating a packet of McCoys and they'd shot out and were lying on the road.

Blue flashing lights. Doors slamming.

Radios going. A serious incident.

Going to shut the road off. Stop the traffic.

Wayne   Stopped the traffic.

Jake (*begins to cry*)   And then . . . I'm so stupid . . .

But I couldn't move me hands. And then . . .

Just stuck. Kept looking down. At the crisps in the blood. Just go. Run. Just go. Go.

But then . . . they looked up.

They all fucking looked up.

Wayne   What?

Jake   They looked up. They looked up and pointed.

Charlie   Idiot!

Jake   Saw me. Caught me. Peering over.

I couldn't move. Legs like lead.

Just stood there.

Pause.

Wayne   We weren't meant to hurt anyone. Were we?

Jake   Blue flashing lights everywhere.

Everywhere.

With them all looking up at me.

All looking up at me.

Charlie   Did they definitely see you, Jake?

Wayne That wasn't meant to happen. We weren't meant to actually hurt anyone. It was meant to fly down, and cars would swerve, just miss it. You know, people driving along would be like 'What the fuck was that! That was close!'

Charlie Did they get a proper look?

Jake Ran. Just ran. Ran. Ran. Lungs hurt but ran and ran. Couldn't see you. I didn't know where you'd gone. You'd gone. Didn't wait. You didn't wait. My guts were twisting and twisting. Ran and ran and ran.

Charlie Twat.

Wayne You're not going anywhere without us.

Charlie 'Course he ain't.

Jake A future. A different place from here.

Wayne Your future's with us.

Jake We can't get nicked for this.

Charlie Oh no. I'm not going down for this. Nor is he. We're gonna say you did it.

Wayne What?

Charlie It was your face they saw. Not mine. Not his.

Jake You can't.

Charlie You looked over the bridge you fucking idiot. It's over mate. It's your fucking little ratty face that they saw gawping over the edge. Your fucking face staring at that twat driving the lorry. Your face they pointed at.

Jake No. No, no, you can't do that. You can't do that.

You can't. You can't do that!

Jake *pushes* **Charlie** *hard, making him drop the knife.* **Jake** *grabs the knife off the mud.*

Wayne Jake, stop it. Put it down.

Jake Fuck. Fuck. Fucking hell.

Charlie (*laughing*)   Look at you, Jake!

Wayne   Stop it you two, we need to hide.

Jake   I've worked too hard. I've worked so fucking hard.

Wayne   Stop it you two, someone will hear us.

Charlie   How does it feel in your hand?

Wayne   Jake, what are you doing?

Jake   I don't know!

Charlie   Can you feel the weight of the handle? Feel it in your hand.

Wayne   Don't do this mate.

Charlie   Do you finally feel alive, Jake?

Wayne   This ain't you.

Charlie   Can you hear the blood pumping round your veins? Is it so fucking loud you feel like your skin's going to rip open?

Wayne   Jake, put the knife down.

Charlie   How does it feel? How does it feel, Jake?

Jake   It feels fucking amazing.

Charlie   See. You are one of us mate.

Enjoy it mate! You enjoy it! Nothing like it.

Jake   What the fuck is going on?

Charlie   How's it feel being a young offender!

Jake   Don't say that. Don't say that.

Charlie   How does it feel to be a number?

Jake   Stop it. Shut up. I got a letter.

Charlie   Looking forward to being strip searched?

Wayne   Do you have to get naked?

Charlie A rubber-gloved hand up your arse?

Wayne You don't do you?

Charlie Having your property taken off you. Put in a clear plastic bag. A little induction to help you cope.

Wayne (*panicking*) Sounds like a laugh! Sounds like a laugh, Jake? We'll all be together. We can look out for each other. We'll be alright.

Charlie I think you'll get quite fond of it when you're there, Jake. It's very . . . comfortable.

Jake I can't . . . I can't . . .

Wayne Leave him alone, Charlie.

Charlie Do you reckon your mum will visit, Jake? I can picture her face. Little tear running down. Cor she's going to be cross with you ain't she! She had big plans for you didn't she. Or disappointed? Oh god she'll be disappointed. Disappointed is worse.

Wayne Don't, Charlie!

Charlie (*to* **Wayne**) What you say? You sticking up for him, Wayne?

Wayne No . . . I just . . .

Jake I ain't going inside.

Charlie Why not? Everyone else does. You're no different. Why do you think you're different? You're as bored as the rest of us. You came out tonight. You got drunk. You ran on to that bridge. There is no way out of this, Jake. This is who we are. We don't leave. We stay. Get a girl pregnant. Get a shit job and we stay. No one gives a fuck about us. That's why we threw that slab off the bridge. To be remembered for *something*.

Jake No you didn't. You did this without thinking. As something to do. Something to fill the time.

Charlie   Look at him. He looks like a man. Do you feel like a man, Jake?

Wayne   Jake, put the knife down.

Jake   Can you imagine what that must have been like. To have that smash into your windscreen. Driving along. Whistling to the radio. Looking forward to his dinner. Thinking about playing with his kids. Maybe he was going to go for a pint with his mates when he got home.

Charlie *spits in* **Jake**'s *face.*

Jake   His missus will have dinner on her own. The kids will sit and cry at their toys and an empty chair will be sat at the table in the pub.

Wayne   Jake, stop it.

Charlie   He was nobody.

Jake   He was somebody's.

Charlie   Shut up!

Jake   You did that. You did that to him.

Wayne   Stop it you two.

Jake   I'm going to be somebody.

Charlie   You can't be. This is who you are.

Charlie *lurches forward and wrestles with* **Jake**. *They both fall to the ground.* **Jake** *drops the knife in the mud.*

Jake   You threw it. Not me. You threw it, Charlie.

You threw it!

You're nothing. You're nobody unless you hurt someone.

Charlie   Shut up.

Jake   That was someone's dad.

Charlie   Shut up before I make you.

Jake ⏐ Someone's dad. Someone's fucking dad!

Wayne *picks up the knife.*

Charlie *wrestles* **Wayne** *for the knife.*

Wayne   Charlie don't. Don't!

Wayne *drops the knife.* **Charlie** *continues to fight* **Wayne**.

Jake *grabs the knife, swings it up into the air and down hard into* **Charlie***'s back.*

Act Two

It is dawn, barely light. The tide is coming in.

Jake, **Wayne** *and* **Charlie** *lie asleep in the mud. Leant up against the wall it is as if they are still hiding from the police and Kirsty's brothers.* **Wayne** *is holding* **Charlie** *in his arms.*

The cold and wet wakes **Jake** *with a start.*

Jake   Wayne. Wake up.

Wayne *wakes and looks at* **Charlie** *in his arms.*

Jake   The tide's coming in.

Pause.

You alright mate?

Wayne *nods.* **Jake** *lights a fag and gives it to* **Wayne**.

Jake   Cold?

I'm freezing.

We need to get up and move about.

Get the blood pumping.

You'll feel better . . . you know . . .

Silence.

Starving. I could do with a great big burger. You know the ones when you bite into them and the grease runs down ya chin. Or chips. You love chips don't you?

Silence.

Wayne   Feel numb.

Pause.

I feel like you do when you wake up in the middle of the night, you sit right up and you're shaking, sweating, you're out of breath and then . . . you remember . . . you remember . . .

Jake   We must have dropped off.

Wayne   He ain't moved. He ain't moved at all.

Jake   Just need to get warm.

Wayne   No. I don't. No. No. I don't want to get warm, I don't want to . . . I just feel . . .

Jake   Why don't we get up and walk about a bit.

Wayne   Why don't you shut up!

Silence.

Jake   The water looks sort of angry don't it?

Racing across the mud.

Like it's coming for us!

Haven't got long.

We have to move soon, Wayne.

Wayne   We'll have to go home.

Jake   Don't know . . .

Wayne   Can't go home.

Jake   Can't go home.

Pause.

Wayne   Why haven't we called an ambulance?

He's still warm, Jake. I think.

He feels warm.

Jake   Can't.

Wayne   We need to get help.

Jake   We can't.

Wayne   I think I can feel his heart. Beating. Faintly.

It's in there. Still banging away inside.

Hold on in there mate. Keep beating Charlie.

He hugs him harder.

I feel like holding him is holding him together.

Like, if I let go . . . if I let go of him . . .

He'll fall apart.

Bits of him lying all over the mud.

Jake   Sun's coming up.

Wayne   Let's just go up there and tell them what we've done and then they can come down here and give him the kiss of life thing and put an oxygen mask on him and put him on a stretcher and I'll keep telling him he'll be alright, you'll be alright Charlie, you'll be alright and they'll take him to hospital.

Jake   He ain't going to hospital. We'll . . . we'll have to leave him here, Wayne. We can't take him with us.

Wayne   We can't leave him here on his own. What, lying here on the mud? No. I ain't doing that. I'm not going anywhere without Charlie. I ain't never done that before. I've never done it. First day of school I went holding his hand and hid behind him as we went into the big hall. I ain't leaving him here lying on the mud.

Jake   That water is getting nearer and nearer mate.

Wayne   Stop saying that. We're not leaving him. You did this. You did this to him. He's lying here on the mud because of you. He's our mate. I know he's a bit of a cunt. I know everyone hates him but . . .

Jake   But what.

Wayne   He makes me laugh more than anyone else I know.

Jake   He doesn't make me laugh.

Wayne Don't lie, Jake. What about the super wedgies he does. He can make boxers turn into a thong quicker than anyone else I know. Stewart Wright in the year below us had to go to the doctors about his ballbag after Charlie had wedgied him so bad. I have never laughed so hard as when I found that out.

Jake That's 'cause Charlie lifted him up by the pants. You should never do that. It's cruel.

He's cruel, mate. I think we are friends with him 'cause we have to be because deep down we're scared of him.

Wayne I ain't scared of him!

Jake We grew up on the same street. Big deal. We don't have to hang out together, for ever.

Wayne If he's as bad as you say why's he been nicking food for me and me brother. Bringing stuff round the house. Putting money in the meter for a bit of electric in the evening. He ain't cruel mate.

Jake . . . then why's he lying there on the mud? Why's he . . . because he is Wayne . . . he is . . .

Wayne He needs help! We need to get him to wake up. Shouldn't have fallen asleep. Open your eyes Charlie. Come on. Wake up! Open your eyes.

Jake Wayne . . .

Wayne Oh god he don't look well. We need to keep him warm. He's getting cold. Oh god, he's so cold, Jake. So cold. Here, have my coat, Charlie.

Jake Don't be so fucking stupid you'll freeze your arse off.

Wayne *takes his coat off and gently puts it over* **Charlie**, *tucking him in tightly.*

Wayne My coat will keep you well warm, Charlie. I wear it in bed sometimes. It's toasty warm.

Jake He don't need your fucking coat, mate.

Wayne   Don't you think he looks sort of comfy now?

I'll look after you, Charlie.

Jake   He don't deserve your coat. He deserves the cold wet mud that he's lying in.

Wayne   Don't say that Jake. Don't say that.

Jake   Sorry.

Wayne   Sleeping. Just sleeping. He looks like he's dreaming. Wonder what he's dreaming of. Probably girls and lots of them.

Jake   I have so many dreams that when I wake up I can never remember any of them.

Wayne   I have day dreams that I work down the docks.

If you work down the docks everyone knows who you are. You're a real man. You have crusty hands and dirt under your nails. You wear ear protectors, a hard hat and a hi-vis. I'd love a hi-vis. And you always have a pint on the way home.

Jake   When that tide comes in it will cover up all the secrets this mud has been keeping.

Wayne   Fucking stinks of hard-boiled eggs. I love eggs.

Jake   Cos it's low in oxygen.

Wayne   What?

Jake   Cos it's low in –

Wayne (*interrupts*)   How the fuck do you know . . .

Jake   *History Magazine*.

Wayne   *History Magazine*?

Jake   The Thames mud is thick. Thick like blancmange.

If you walk in too far. You start to sink.

I mean really sink. Quickly an' all.

Sometimes, I dare myself to go out further dreading that today will be the day that I can't get back.

Wondering if today will be the day . . .

Pause.

Wayne Do you really read the *History Magazine*?

Jake What do you want to do with your life, Wayne?

Wayne What the fuck kind of question is that?

Jake What do you want out of it?

Wayne What?

Jake To achieve?

Wayne (*thinks*) More pubes. I wish I had more. I'd love a great big bush of them. Imagine how manly I would be in me hard hat, hi-vis and a big bush of pubes.

What do you want?

Jake I want a metal detector.

Wayne What! A metal detector? Can't believe you still want one. I always thought that was a bit of a joke.

Jake I really want one.

Wayne Does that mean you've got loads of pubes then?

Jake *doesn't answer.*

A metal detector?

Jake Just think it would be good.

Wayne You'd look like a dick!

Jake So would you with a great big bush of hair popping out of your boxers.

Wayne Women would love it! Me and Charlie would be pulling birds left right and centre.

Jake I'd be rich. I'd find stuff. Bounty.

Wayne   Ain't that a chocolate bar?

Jake   Shut up!

Wayne   You'd only pick up shit from round here, mate.

Jake   Things from the past.

Wayne   You'd fucking catch something. Grow another leg.
Germ central.

Jake   Precious artefacts /

Wayne   Arte-what??

Jake   They would be priceless and have to be kept up at the
British Museum.

Wayne   What's that then?

Jake   Beep. Beep. Beep.

Wayne   Do you fink Charlie's alright? He still ain't moved.

Jake   Beep. Beep. Beep.

Wayne   Should we have done the recovery position thing?

Jake   Beep. Beep . . . Bingo!

Everything's changed. You've struck gold.

You can buy whatever you want.

You can go wherever you want.

You can get the fuck out of here.

Wayne   I like it here.

Jake   Do you ever dare yourself to do stuff?

Wayne   Not really.

Jake   Don't you get urges? Urges to jump into the water.
Step in front of a car?

Wayne   What?

Jake   Me muscles twitch. As if to go. Jump. Me muscles are ready. Braver than me head. Me head always wins. It's like falling down the stairs in a dream, that jerk as you wake up!

Wayne   Charlie was right about you.

Jake   I dare myself to do stuff all the time.

Wayne   You're a loser. That's why you looked over the bridge tonight.

Jake *jumps up and starts miming walking along with a metal detector.*

Jake   My metal detector.

Beeb, beeb, beeb.

If my house was burning down, I'd go back in, through the fire and get it.

Even if they said we can't.

I'd fight back the flames.

I'd love my metal detector.

Beeb, beeb, beeb.

It beeps when something good is about to happen.

Finds me treasures I can keep!

Over here! Look in the ground. Dig it out!

We're going to get out of 'ere.

One little bit of metal out the mud.

Fame and fortunes.

We'll wave as we go, me and my metal detector.

Wayne   You're a loser with a fucking metal detector.

Jake   It would be my ticket out of here. To go somewhere else. Live somewhere else. Be someone else. Fucking hell, Wayne, don't you ever wonder?

Wayne   No.

Jake   I think about it all the time. Different weather.

Wayne   I've heard it's cold up north.

Jake   Different streets.

Wayne   Probably need more than me bobble hat to sleep in.

Jake   Different accents.

Wayne   I s'pose I'd like Liverpool. Go and see the game every week.

Jake   Different people.

Wayne   What's wrong wiv round 'ere?

Pause.

Jake   It's not a great view is it?

Wayne   It's alright . . .

Jake   There's nothing to look at. Other parts of the country they have things to look at. Mountains, cliffs, the ocean. What have we got? Kent.

Wayne   Have you been hanging out with your nan or something? It might not be pretty, but it's ours. This is our view. I'm proud of it.

Jake   We have got nothing.

Wayne   It's our home. Alright, we ain't got a premiership football club. That's pretty shit. We've got everything else though. We've got everything we need to be happy.

Jake   What? Shipping containers, cranes, chimneys wiv smoke billowing out. Our lungs must have a black lining from the crap we have to breathe in every day.

Wayne   I like it. When the air smells of washing powder from the factories I feel all clean.

Jake   This town sits on the bend of the river and has picked up the crap that has washed ashore since the day it was formed.

Wayne   Charlie thinks it's shit down here.

Jake   The grey sky mixes into the grey town and the grey docks and the grey cranes and the grey machinery.

Wayne   I love hearing the noise of the containers crashing down on to the ships late at night.

Jake   If I could swim across there I would.

Wayne   The metal thuds at night remind ya someone is out in the cold loading that on. Someone is working while you're tucked up in bed. It's lovely.

They listen and sure enough there is the sound of a container crashing down on to a ship.

I've had to sleep in three pairs of socks this week. Me Liverpool bobble hat and put the rug off the floor on top. I've been so cold I share the bed with me brother. I've never had to turn the boiler on before either. Do you know how to turn a boiler on?

Jake   What's going on, Wayne?

Wayne   And the electric keeps running out. Not so bad as the street light right outside means you can pretty much see everything. Me little brother gets well bored though. What's a six-year-old meant to do with no telly?

Jake   Has something happened to your dad?

Wayne   I quite like sleeping in me bobble hat as it makes me feel all toasty but wearing it all day and sleeping in it is making it smell a bit funny.

Jake   Don't you wish we could get on one of them containers? Look! That one's going to China. We could go to China.

Wayne   What, go on the run? Eat out of bins. Grow great big beards and wear carrier bags round our feet as shoes.

Jake   We could row our way to safety. Follow the ship to China.

Wayne   I don't really like noodles though.

Jake   Or we could go up the river, following the twinkling lights along the shore until we get to London.

Wayne   I ain't going anywhere.

Jake   More and more lights appear as you approach the city. Flashing in the sky and on the top of fucking massive skyscrapers.

They have so much money up there they leave the lights on all night.

Their streets, wrists and phones covered in gold. It's the place to be. Follow the river and it will show you the way to the big smoke!

Jake *runs and jumps into the old derelict boat. He beckons for* **Wayne** *to join him.*

Jake   Come on!

Wayne   What you doing?

Jake   We're getting out of here.

Wayne   You've gone mental.

Jake   We're escaping.

Wayne   This boat can't take us anywhere. It's got holes in it. And it's tiny. The container ships would . . . well they would . . .

Jake   We could get dragged out to sea but who cares. We would bob along till we get to France.

Wayne   Can't go there, can't speak the language and I hate garlic.

Jake *offers* **Wayne** *a piece of wood that resembles an oar.*

Jake   You can drive.

Wayne   I ain't playing stupid games.

Jake   Bet you always have to sit in the back with your brother don't you.

Wayne   We ain't even got a car.

Jake   Things don't always have to be the same, Wayne. Things can change. You don't have to sit in the back watching for ever. One day. You can drive.

Wayne *takes the oar and steps into the boat.* **Jake** *points out things as they pretend to float past them.*

Jake   This is the most dangerous part of the journey. Negotiating our way around fifty-foot-high tankers and cruisers.

Wayne   This is stupid.

Jake   They can't see us. But we can see them. The massive waves from the tankers make the boat shake from side to side.

Jake *makes the boat shake.*

Wayne   Stop it, I feel sick. I think I'm going to have to close my eyes.

Jake   The air is thick from the smoke from the oil refineries –

Wayne   The what?

Jake   Chemicals fill the air as we pass under the huge Dartford crossing.

Wayne *opens his eyes to look.*

Wayne   Can we see Lakeside?

Jake   Watch out! Here comes one of them discos on a boat, full of rich people. Wave at them!

Jake *and* **Wayne** *do large 'wanker' signs.*

Jake   Come on, Wayne. Let's get out of here.

Wayne *begins to punt along.*

Jake   Quick through this bit. It's all shit along here. Factories, sewage works, waste management depots.

Wayne   Stinks.

Jake   Come on Wayne, row faster.

Wayne   Why do I have to do it? It's hurting me arms.

Jake   Until, suddenly, the Thames Barrier.

Wayne   Wow!

Wayne *stops rowing and they stare up at the imaginary Thames Barrier.*

Wayne   What is it?

Jake   Dunno. But it signals that we're nearly there.

Wayne   Nearly where?

Jake   On our left, the majestic crown that is the Millennium Dome.

Wayne   Charlie's mum went to see Enrique there.

Jake   Come on Wayne, row. We have to go right round it.

They both lean right imagining going round the Dome.

Jake   To our right, Canary Wharf, ladies and gentlemen. Where money is made. Where the rich people live.

Wayne   Do people live there?

Jake   It's like something out of a film. A new civilisation. Shiny bits of metal sticking out the land. The future, Wayne.

Wayne   I can see Canary Wharf from the roof of Charlie's flat.

Jake   I think I'd like to live there. It looks . . . clean. Modern.

They both stare up as if the building disappears into the sky.

Wayne   Can you row now?

Jake (*ignores him*)   Greenwich.

Wayne   Well posh!

Jake   And the *Cutty Sark*. The old tea clipper.

Wayne   I've always wondered what that looks like. Can you go on it?

Jake   Did you know that she crashed into a Royal Navy ship on the Thames and the figurehead lost one of its arms. It bobbed along downstream waving at everything it passed until it washed up on our beach. Did you know that!

Wayne   Arrghh! Is that a whale?

Jake   Don't be stupid. It's the Thames not the Atlantic.

Wayne   There was one before, I saw it on the telly.

Jake (*shouts*)   Duck!

They both duck.

Jake (*shouts*)   Tower Bridge!

Wayne   Wow! It's beautiful.

Jake   To your right, the Tower of London.

Wayne   I remember we went there on a school trip because I was sick on the coach trip back. I had to do it into a carrier bag. Do you remember? It fucking stunk!

Jake   HMS *Belfast*.

Wayne   What's that?

Jake   A big Navy ship. Used in the Second World War.

Wayne   Boring.

Jake   Next, the London Eye.

Wayne   It's going very slowly. I reckon you'd have more fun on the big wheel down Southend. At least you're out in the open so you can throw chips at people.

Jake   The Houses of Parliament.

Wayne   Big Ben innit?

Jake   And the politicians are all out on their balcony, clinking their champagne glasses.

They mime clinking their glasses and fake laughing.

Wayne   What does a politician do?

Jake   Decides things about the country. Debates about stuff. They make changes to things. They can make things happen.

Wayne   What's next? What's next!

Jake   I dunno. I think it might be another bridge or something. The river goes somewhere but . . . We don't belong round the next bit. Think that's the end of the story.

Wayne *screams as he falls overboard on to the mud.*

Wayne   We've hit something.

Jake   What you doing?

Wayne   I think it's an iceberg!

Jake (*laughing*)   Man overboard, man overboard!

Jake *grabs the piece of wood and frantically mimes paddling.*

Wayne   I'm hanging on to the boat with my fingertips.

Jake   No point. A surge of water takes you.

Jake *hits* **Wayne**'s *fingers with his paddle.*

Wayne   Fuck! What do you do that for!

Jake   Gone. An undertow grabs your legs and you're under.

Wayne   A what? What's an undertow?

Jake   You're under the water and you can't breathe and you can't see because the water is so dirty /

Wayne   Am I drowning then?

Jake   Some gets in your mouth and you've never tasted anything so rank and /

Wayne   Why am I drowning? I don't want to be the one that drowns.

Jake   Gone. Washed out to sea. Never seen again.

Wayne   That really hurt, Jake!

Jake   And I have to go back up there and tell them all what's happened. Tell them you and Charlie threw that bit of concrete over that bridge.

Wayne   Shit, stop it Jake. Stop it. Let me back on the boat.

Jake   And tell them . . .

Wayne   Let me back on Jake. The tide's coming in, me feet are wet.

Jake   And tell them that you knifed Charlie.

Wayne   I can feel water in me shoes.

Jake   That you did it. Can I say you did it?

Wayne   I think me shoe's stuck.

Jake   I have plans you know. You have nothing. Nothing.

Wayne   Stop it, Jake. My shoe's come off. Stop it.

Jake   Can I tell them you knifed Charlie?

Will you say you did it? I need you to say you did it.

Pause.

Wayne   The water will hit Charlie soon.

It might wake him up?

Jake   Please, Wayne?

Pause.

Wayne   I think we should go. Let's go and say we need help for our friend. Together.

Jake *doesn't answer him.*

Wayne   Let's go up there together.

Jake   The tide. Shit. Get on the wall.

Jake *jumps on to the riverwall.* **Wayne** *runs towards* **Charlie**.

Wayne   Come on, mate. The tide's come in. You're getting wet. We're going to get you out of here.

Wayne *desperately tries to move* **Charlie**.

Jake   Leave him.

Wayne   I can't do it. He's too heavy. I can't move him. I can't move him.

Jake   You have to leave him.

Wayne   I think the water's got into the coat. He's so heavy. I can't lift him. He needs help, Jake. We've got to get him help. Look at him. He's got blood all dried into his jeans. It's in his hair.

Jake   Wayne. He's . . . We can't help him.

Wayne   I can't leave him. Why don't you fucking understand that?! He's so cold. So cold. I'm going to give him me bobble hat.

Jake   Don't!

Wayne *tenderly takes his bobble hat off and puts it on* **Charlie**.

Jake   Get over here. It's fucking dangerous down there. The water is really coming in now. You've got to get up here. Now!

Wayne (*gently*)   Come on, Charlie.

Jake   Wayne, you need to get off that mud and get on this wall!

Wayne   Please, Jake. I need your help. I can't move him on me own. I need you to come and help me.

Jake   No.

Wayne   Please, Jake. I can't leave him here.

Jake   No.

Pause.

Wayne   I'm sorry, Charlie. I'm sorry.

Jake   One surge, Wayne. One powerful current. You're gone mate. It will take you!

Wayne   It's getting light now. It'll warm up soon. You've got me bobble hat. We're over the worst of it, Charlie. We'll be alright. We'll get you help.

Jake   Come out of the water, Wayne. You need to get out of the water.

Wayne   Look at the colour of his face. It's like he's got no blood left. It's like he's, it's like he's . . . Has he gone, Jake? Has he . . . gone? Fuck!

Wayne *starts crying.*

The tide has come in and the water is rising.

Jake   I thought we were going to do this together? Don't leave me up here, mate. I can't do this on me own.

Wayne   I can't!

Jake   You can't stay with him.

Wayne   I can't move.

Jake   Stop mucking about. We can't muck about any more. Why are you doing this? He's not worth it.

Wayne   I can't move. The more you shout about it the more my feet are fucking sinking. Jake!

Jake   Grab my hand.

Wayne   You'll help me, but not him!

Jake   I can't reach you!

Wayne   Me legs are stuck! I'm sinking into the mud.

Jake   Fucking hell. Grab my arm.

Wayne   I can't! What about Charlie? I can't! What about Charlie? What about Charlie?

Jake *hangs off the wall and reaches for* **Wayne***. Slowly he drags him up and on to the wall.*

Wayne   Oh my god. He's floating, Jake. He's fucking floating. Is he going to float away?

Jake   I don't know mate. Probably.

Wayne   Will he float out to sea? I have to get him.

Jake   You can't go back in mate. It's too dangerous.

Wayne   I thought he was alright. I thought he was going to be alright. I thought . . . when I held him . . . he was shivering 'cause he was cold. I thought huddling up together . . . I thought we'd be alright.

He was gurgling and gasping for air and I just held him. I shouldn't have held him should I? I always do the wrong thing. We should have gone for help.

Jake   But we didn't.

Wayne   We fell asleep.

Jake   We did nothing.

Pause.

Wayne   You killed Charlie.

Jake   You killed that man.

*They stand and watch **Charlie**'s body bob about, slowly drifting away.*

Wayne   Least he's got my coat on.

Jake   And your bobble hat.

Wayne   And me bobble hat.

Jake   He'll be toasty warm, mate. Toasty warm.

Wayne   I want to be toasty warm.

Jake   Me too mate. Me too.

Pause.

Wayne   This morning I woke up 'cause me brother was . . .

No sign of Dad. Bed not slept in.

Thought he might be on the lounge floor.

Still pissed from the night before.

He's often on the lounge floor in the morning.

Lying there in his coat.

Just for a minute you think he's dead.

He wasn't and me brother was still . . .

Dad's wardrobe was empty. Drawers empty.

And me brother's still . . .

Thought . . . guess he's fucked off then.

The fridge ain't got nothing in it.

Didn't know what to do.

And me brother . . . me brother was still crying.

Jake I'm sorry, Wayne.

Wayne Half a loaf and some cans of beer.

I was surprised he didn't take them with him.

I don't know if we'll notice that he's gone.

It's been like he's gone for ages.

Jake Where's your little brother?

Wayne Left him there.

They pause, digesting what he's said.

Jake He's probably burnt the house down.

Wayne Probably.

Jake There'll probably be people waiting for ya.

Wayne I know.

Jake Social will probably split you up.

Wayne I know.

Suddenly the lights from several police cars can be seen in the distance.

Jake I can't go up there. I can't . . .

Wayne We have to. I have to go home. Come on . . .

Jake I can't.

Wayne We have to mate.

Jake Can't.

Wayne We have to tell 'em what we've done.

Jake I don't know what I was thinking.

Dreaming of . . . Fucking dreams.

Wayne There's nothing to do round here.

It's just what happens . . .

What are we supposed to do?

Jake Drift along. Make do. Have a laugh.

Wayne You need to put your hand up when you've fucked up.

Jake Doesn't always work though, does it?

Wayne We'll be alright, mate.

The sound of the sirens is getting nearer.

Jake When I look up there I see my mum's face.

Wayne I see me brother's. I have to make sure he's going to be alright. I'm all he's got.

Jake She was so proud of me.

Wayne Proud of what?

Jake I got a letter this morning. I got in.

Wayne Got in? Got in where?

Jake *starts to cry.*

Jake   She's spent so much money on getting all the books for me.

Wayne   What books?

Jake   I was celebrating tonight. It was my big night.

Wayne   What you talking about mate?

Jake   They accepted me.

Wayne   You been going school? You going college? You're going sixth-form college?

Jake   I sat all my exams. I'd done all right. I know it. I've worked hard. I've worked so fucking hard.

Wayne   You did your exams? You revised? Fuck off did ya! This ain't you. What the fuck would you do at college? What would me and Charlie do?

Jake   Never know now. Never know.

Pause.

Wayne   Time to stop playing . . .

Jake *walks right to the edge of the riverwall.*

Wayne   Careful, Jake. Don't do that.

It's got deep, ain't it?

Come away from the edge, mate.

The water has come in well quick.

Looks cold don't it. Murky brown.

Come away from the edge, Jake.

Making me feel sick. Legs are going a bit.

Can't see Charlie now.

Can you see Charlie?

Can't see Charlie no more.

Is he still there?

Has he gone, Jake? Has he gone?

He's gone, ain't he?

Won't see him again, will we?

Jake *shakes his head.*

Wayne   Bye mate. Take care. Miss ya.

Pause.

It's over ain't it?

It's over ain't it, Jake?

Jake   No other way.

Wayne   We'll do this together.

Jake   We'll do this together.

Jake *holds out his hand and* **Wayne** *grabs hold of it. They stand on the wall for a few moments. Suddenly* **Jake** *jumps but* **Wayne** *lets go and stays where he is.*

There is a splash. **Jake** *has gone.*

The flashing lights of the police cars fall on **Wayne**'s *face.*

The end.